THE WORLD'S FUNNIEST
ANIMAL JOKES
For Kids

First published in Great Britain in 2002 by
Dean, an imprint of Egmont Books Limited,
239 Kensington High Street,
London W8 6SA

Copyright © 2002 Egmont Books Limited

ISBN 0 603 56064 4

1 3 5 7 9 10 8 6 4 2

Printed and bound in the U.A.E.

THE WORLD'S FUNNIEST ANIMAL JOKES
For Kids

Written and Compiled by: Guy Campbell & Mark Devins
Illustrated by: Paul Moran & Simon Ecob

What do Paddington, Rupert and Pooh pack when they go on holiday?
Just the bear essentials!

How do you get six donkeys in a fire engine?
Two in the front, two in the back and two on the top going "Heehaw Heehaw Heehaw"!

What do you get if you cross a centipede and a chicken?
Enough drumsticks to feed an army!

A man walks into a pub with a tiger.
"Do you serve Welsh people in here?"
he asks the barman.
"Certainly, Sir." the barman replies.
"Good. A pint for me, then, please, and two Welsh people for the tiger..."

What happened when the chef found a daddy long legs in the salad?
It became a daddy short legs!

What do ants take when they're ill?
Anty Biotics!

What is a newly hatched beetle?
A baby buggy!

A little turtle begins to climb a tree slowly. After long hours of great effort, he reaches the top, jumps into the air, waving his front legs frantically, then crashes heavily into the ground. After recovering consciousness, he starts to climb the tree again, jumps once more, but again crashes to the ground. The little turtle does this again and again, while all the time his heroic efforts are being watched with sadness by a couple of birds perched on a nearby branch. Finally, the female bird says to the male bird,
"Dear, don't you think it's time to tell Tommy he is adopted?"

What do you get if you cross a glow worm with a python?
A 15-foot strip light that can strangle you to death!

Where did Noah keep his bees?
In the ark hives!

What do you call a vet with laryngitis?
A hoarse doctor!

How do you change tyres on a duck?
With a quackerjack!

What does Tarzan say when he sees a herd of elephants in the distance?
"Look, a herd of elephants in the distance!"

What does Tarzan say when he sees a herd of elephants wearing sunglasses in the distance?
Nothing. He doesn't recognise them!

Why shouldn't you take bears to the zoo?
Because they'd rather go to the cinema!

**What noise does a cat make
going down the motorway?**
Miaoooooooooooooooooooooooooooooooow!

**What is the difference between a flea-bitten
dog and a bored visitor?**
One's going to itch and the other
is itching to go!

**Hickory dickory dock,
the mice ran up the clock.
The clock struck one,**
the rest got away with minor injuries!

**A penguin walks into a bar and
says to the barman,
"Have you seen my Dad?"
"I don't know," says the barman.**
"What does he look like?"

A man and his dog sat in a movie hall, both enjoying a movie. When the film ended, the dog applauded until his paws were sore. The man sitting on the next seat was wonderstruck.
"That's amazing!" he exclaimed.
"Yes, it is," agreed the dog owner.
"He hated the book..."

What do you get if you cross a cat with a parrot?
A carrot!

What's big, grey and mutters?
A mumbo jumbo!

Where do monkeys make toast?
Under a gorilla!

How do we know elephants are always unhappy?
Because of their great sighs!

How do bees get to school?
By school buzz!

11

Last time David went to the zoo he got into trouble for feeding the monkeys...
He fed them to the lions!

What do you call a woodpecker with no beak?
A headbanger!

What is green, sooty and whistles when it rubs its back legs together?
Chimney Cricket!

Where do you weigh a whale?
At the whale-weigh station!

What do you call a vampire's dog?
A werewoof!

What do you get if you cross a skunk with a boomerang?
A horrendous smell that keeps coming back!

A duck walks into a pharmacy and says "Got any bread?" The pharmacist explains he has no bread because it is a pharmacy. Then he tells the duck to try the supermarket nearby. Fifteen minutes later the duck comes back and says, "Got any bread?" The pharmacist again tells the duck he doesn't sell bread and to try another shop around the corner. A few minutes later the duck is back again and says, "Got any bread?" The pharmacist screams that if the duck asks him for bread one more time he will nail its bill to the floor. The duck leaves. Twenty minutes later the duck comes back. "Got any nails?" he says. The pharmacist explains that NO, being a PHARMACIST, he doesn't sell NAILS either. "Oh," says the duck, "in that case... Got any bread?"

What do you get if you cross a tiger with a kangaroo?
A stripey jumper!

A baby blackbird fell out of its nest and went flying through the branches of the oak tree towards the ground. "Are you all right?" called out a magpie as the chick went hurtling past his perch. "So far!" said the little bird.

What do Alexander the Great and Winnie-the-Pooh have in common? They both have "the" as their middle names!

A tortoise is mugged one day by a gang of snails. The police asked him what his attackers looked like and he said, "I really don't know, it all happened so fast!"

What's black, yellow and covered in blackberries? A bramble bee!

**What has ten guns
and terrifies the ocean?**
Billy the squid!

What has six legs, four ears, two trunks and three tusks?
An elephant with spares!

What's brown and sees just as well from either end?
A horse with its eyes shut!

Why do elephants have grey skin?
To keep their insides from falling out!

Why aren't elephants allowed on beaches?
They can't keep their trunks up!

Why did they make two Yogi Bears?
Because they made a Boo-Boo with the first one!

What do you get if you cross an elephant with the abominable snowman?
A jumbo yeti!

What has antlers and sucks blood?
A moose-quito!

What's grey and wrinkled and lights up?
An electric elephant!

**What did one centipede say to the
other centipede?**
You've got a lovely pair of legs, you've got a
lovely pair of legs, you've got a lovely pair of
legs, you've got a lovely pair of legs...!

What did the bee say to the naughty bee?
Bee-hive yourself!

Why do elephants have big ears?
Because Noddy wouldn't pay the ransom!

**A man goes into a pet shop and asks to buy
a wasp. The shopkeeper tells him they don't
sell wasps. "That's strange," says the man.**
"You had one in the window yesterday!"

What does a caterpillar do on New Year's Day?
Turns over a new leaf!

Which fly makes films?
Stephen Speilbug!

What's pretty, delicate and carries a machine-gun?
A killer butterfly!

Why didn't the two worms get on Noah's Ark in an apple?
Because everyone had to go on in pears!

What do you get if you cross a fish and a Ducati?
A motor pike!

Why don't centipedes play football?
Because by the time they've got their boots on, it's time to go home!

What wears glass slippers and weighs a ton?
Cinderelephant!

A Shaggy Dog Story

A local business looking for office help
put a sign in the window saying:
"HELP WANTED. Must be able to type,
must be good with a computer
and be bilingual".
A short time later, a dog trotted up to the
window, saw the sign and went inside.
He looked at the receptionist and wagged
his tail, then walked over to the sign,
looked at it and whined.
Getting the idea, the receptionist got the
office manager. The office manager
looked at the dog and was surprised, to
say the least. However, since the dog
looked determined, he led him into the
office. Inside, the dog jumped up on
the chair and stared at the
manager, who said,
"I can't hire you.

You have to be able to type."
The dog jumped down, went to the typewriter and typed out a perfect letter. He took out the page and trotted over to the manager, gave it to him and then jumped back on the chair. The manager was stunned, but then reminded the dog, "The sign says you have to be good with a computer." The dog jumped down again and went to the computer. He then demonstrated his expertise with various programs, producing a sample spreadsheet and database. By this time, the manager was totally dumbfounded! He looked at the dog and said, "I realise that you are a very intelligent dog and have some fantastic abilities. However, I still can't give you the job. The sign also says that you have to be bilingual."
The dog looked him straight in the face, and said, "Meow."

What do you call a camel with three humps?
Humphrey!

Why is a baseball team like fish and chips?
They both need a decent batter!

What do you get when you put a fish and an elephant together?
Swimming trunks!

What has four wheels and flies?
A wheelie bin!

What do you call a cow with no sense of direction?
Udderly lost!

What do you get if you cross a skunk with an elephant?
A smell you never forget!

What do you get if you cross a cow with a crystal ball?
A message from the udder side!

How do snails get their shells so shiny?
Snail varnish!

Why did the fly fly?
Because the spider spied 'er!

How can you get a set of teeth put in for free?
Smack a lion!

If a four-legged animal is a quadruped and a two-legged animal is a biped, what's a tiger?
A stri-ped!

What do you call a lion who has eaten your mother's sister?
An aunt-eater!

What do you get if you cross a rabbit and a flea?
Bugs Bunny!

Why do sea-gulls fly over the sea?
Because if they flew over the bay
they would be bagels!

**What do you get if you cross a toad
with a mist?**
Kermit the Fog!

What do insects learn at school?
Mothematics!

How do you start a bug race?
One, two, flea - go!

**What is the difference between a flea
and a wolf?**
One prowls on the hairy and the other howls
on the prairie!

**What happened at the badly organised cow
milking contest?**
It was udder chaos...

How do fleas travel?
Itch hiking!

What kind of key opens a banana?
A monkey!

What is a myth?
A female moth!

**A salesman dropped in to see
a business customer.
No one was in the office except
a big dog emptying wastebaskets.
The salesman stared at the animal,
wondering if his imagination could
be playing tricks on him.
The dog looked up and said,
"Don't be surprised. This is just part of
my job." "Incredible!" exclaimed the man.
"I can't believe it! Does your boss
know what a prize he has in you,
an animal that can talk?"**

"Don't tell him that!" said the dog.
"If he finds out I can talk, he'll make me
answer the phone as well!"

Why were the flies playing football in a saucer?
They were playing for the cup!

Why can't two elephants go swimming?
Because they have only one pair of trunks between them!

A Polar Bear cub says to his mum: "Mum, are you sure I'm a Polar Bear?" "Yes, of course, Darling. Why would you ask me that?" The little bear says:
"Because I'm absolutely FREEZING!"

What do worms leave round their baths?
The scum of the earth!

When is the best time to buy budgies?
When they're going cheap!

What do butterflies sleep on?
Caterpillows!

What did the earwig skydiver say as it jumped out of the plane?
Earwig go!

What is the definition of a caterpillar?
A worm in a fur coat!

**How come if ants are always
so busy they always get
time to show up at picnics?**

What is smaller than an ant's mouth?
An ant's dinner!

**What do you get if you cross a
pony and a detective?**
Inspector Horse!

What says "Quick, Quick"?
A duck with hiccups!

What's green and loud?
A froghorn!

What is a little dog's favourite drink?
Pupsi-cola!

A crab is sitting on the ocean floor when a lobster comes up to him dragging a half-dead octopus. The octopus is coughing, very pale and has a nasty rash.
The lobster says to the crab:
"Alright, mate, here's that sick squid
I owe you."

What does a flamingo do when it rains?
It gets wet!

What do you call a pony with a sore throat?
A little horse!

Why did the dolphin cross the beach?
To get to the other tide!

What do ducks watch on TV?
Duckumentaries!

What do whales eat?
Fish and ships!

Why did the crab get arrested?
Because he was always pinching things!

Why wouldn't they let the butterfly into the dance?
Because it was a moth ball!

What do you get when you cross a parrot with a monster?
A creature that gets a cracker whenever it asks for one!

It was a boring Sunday afternoon in the jungle so the Elephants decided to challenge the Ants to a game of soccer. The game was going well with the Elephants beating the Ants ten goals to nil, when the Ants gained possession. The Ants' star player was dribbling the ball towards the Elephants' goal when the Elephants' left back came lumbering towards him.

The Elephant trod on the little Ant, killing him instantly. The referee stopped the game. "What the hell do you think you're doing? Do you call that sportsmanship, killing another player?" The Elephant replied, "Well, I didn't mean to kill him...
I was just trying to trip him up!"

Why did the parrot wear a raincoat?
Because she wanted to be Polly
unsaturated!

**What did the gamekeeper say to the
lord of the manor?**
"The pheasants are revolting!"

When does a cart come before a horse?
In the dictionary!

**How does a queen bee get
around her hive?**
She's throne!

**What do you get if you cross a dinosaur
with a dog?**
Tyrannnosaurus Rex!

**What kind of snack do little monkeys
have with their milk?**
Chocolate chimp cookies!

This kangaroo escaped his enclosure at London Zoo. After recapturing the kangaroo, the zookeeper put up a ten-foot fence round the enclosure. Next morning, the kangaroo was out again, roaming around the zoo. So the fence was extended to 20 feet high. Next morning, sure enough, the kangaroo is out again. Frustrated, the zoo officials built the fence 40 feet high. A camel in the next enclosure asked the kangaroo, "Gee, how much higher do you think they'll go?" The kangaroo said, "About a 1,000 feet I guess, unless somebody starts locking the gate..."

What does a queen bee do when she burps?
Issues a royal pardon!

What do whales like to chew?
Blubber gum!

Where does Duck Lightyear go?
To infinity, and the pond!

What do horses play when they're bored?
Stable tennis!

What do you call a bee born in May?
A maybe!

Two escaped lions are walking through a city centre. One says:
"Quiet today, isn't it?"

What do parrots eat?
Polyfilla!

What's the difference between a worm and an apple?
Have you ever tried worm pie?

There was an old man in France who used to get up every morning at five a.m. He would then go and sprinkle a white powder on the roads. When a passing policeman asked him

what he was sprinkling on the roads, he answered that it was elephant powder. The policeman scoffed, "But everybody knows that there are no elephants in France!" and the old man said,

"You see, it works!"

The world's funniest **ANIMAL JOKES**

What did one worm say to the other when he was late home?
Where in earth have you been?

What kind of doorbell do bees have?
A hum dinger!

Why are elephants wrinkly?
Because they hate being ironed!

A snake says to his Mother, "Mum, am I poisonous?"
"Why do you ask, love?" says his Mum.
"I've just bitten my tongue!"

What happened when the cat swallowed a coin?
There was some money in the kitty!

Customer: This fish isn't cooked.
Waiter: How do you know?
Customer: It's eaten all my chips!

What happens when it rains cats and dogs?
You step in a poodle!

How do you start a teddy bear race?
Ready, teddy, go!

What do you give a sick budgie?
Tweetment!

What goes hum-choo, hum-choo?
A bee with a cold!

Why do elephants have trunks?
Because they would look silly with glove compartments!

Why did the turtle cross the road?
To get to the Shell garage!

What should you do if you are suddenly chased by a big pink bird?
Flamin' Go!

Why did the chicken cross the playground?
To get to the other slide!

What goes "Hith Hith"?
A snake with a lisp!

What's black and white and makes a lot of noise?
A zebra with a drum kit!

Why don't elephants wear shoes?
They can't tie the laces on their back feet when they have shoes on their front feet!

What goes zzub, zzub?
A bee flying backwards!

What did the bee say to the other bee in summer?
Swarm here isn't it?

What do you call a cat that has just eaten a whole duck?

A duck-filled fatty puss!

A frog goes to see a fortune teller and is told, "You are going to meet a beautiful young girl who will want to know everything about you."
The frog says, "This is great! Will I meet her at a party, or what?"
"No," says the psychic.
"In her biology class."

How did Bo Peep lose her sheep?
She had a crook with her!

Why don't elephants like turnips?
For the same reasons that people don't like turnips!

What's the difference between a fish and a piano?
You can't tuna fish!

What do you call a pig with three eyes?
A piiig!

What happens when geese land in a volcano?
They cook their own gooses!

How do you find where a flea has bitten you?
Start from scratch!

What did the teddy bear say to the waiter when he offered him some pudding?
No thanks. I'm stuffed!

Have you ever seen a man-eating tiger?
No, but in the café next door I once saw a man eating chicken!

What is a Twip?
It's when wabbits twavel!

What's the difference between a rabbit that runs and a rabbit that goes "Kalaka Hoo Ha!"
One's a fit bunny and the other's a bit funny!

Customer: When I bought this cat, you told me he was good for mice. He won't go near them!
Shopkeeper: Well, isn't that good for mice?

What do you get from a drunk chicken?
Scotch eggs!

What does a bee get at McDonalds?
A humburger!

Which side of a chicken has the most feathers?
The outside!

Why don't elephants wear high heels?
They think they already have pretty ankles!

What do you get if you cross a cow with a grass cutter?
A lawn mooer!

What do you get when giraffes collide?
A giraffic jam!

What insect is good for you?
Vitamin bee!

How can you tell if an elephant is getting ready to charge?
He pulls out his American Express card!

What looks like half a cat?
The other half!

What do you call a big Irish spider?
Paddy long legs!

What do you call a bald teddy?
Fred bear!

Why are igloos round?
So penguins can't hide in the corners!

How do you know when there's an elephant under the bed?
Your nose is touching the ceiling!

What is green and pecks on trees?
Woody Wood Pickle!

Why did the bees go on strike?
They wanted more honey and
shorter flowers!

**How can you tell if an elephant has used
your toothbrush?**
It smells of peanuts!

**What happened when the boy jellyfish
met the girl jellyfish?**
Jelly babies!

What goes 99-clonk, 99-clonk, 99-clonk?
A centipede with a wooden leg!

**What do you call a rabbit wearing a
blue and white scarf?**
A Chelsea Bun!

Upon entering the little village shop, a tourist noticed a sign saying "DANGER! BEWARE OF DOG!" posted on the glass door. Inside he noticed a harmless old hounddog asleep on the floor beside the cash register. He asked the shop manager, "Is that the dog folks are supposed to beware of?" "Yep, that's him," the manager replied.
The stranger looked amused.
"That old thing? He's got no teeth and he must be 35 years old! Why in the world would you put up a sign saying 'Danger! Beware of the dog'?"
"Because," the owner replied, "before I put that sign up, people kept tripping over him."

How can you tell if you are looking at a police glow worm?
It has a blue flashing light!

The Tramp and the Hamster

A tramp goes into a restaurant and orders a burger. The waiter says, "No way. I don't think you can pay for it." The tramp says, "You're right. I don't have any money, but if I show you something you have never seen before, will you give it to me?" The waiter agrees, and the tramp reaches into his pocket, and pulls out a hamster. The hamster runs to the end of the counter, climbs down to the floor, runs across the room, and gets up on to the piano and starts playing Elton John tunes. The waiter says, "Wow, that hamster is a really good piano player!" He brings the tramp a burger, which he eats, and he asks for another. "Money or another miracle," says the waiter. The tramp reaches into his coat again and pulls out a frog. He puts the frog on the counter, and the frog starts to sing Ricky

Martin songs brilliantly. A stranger from the other end of the counter runs over to the tramp and offers him a hundred pounds for the frog. The tramp says, "OK", and takes the money. The stranger takes the frog and runs out of the restaurant. The waiter says, "Are you crazy? You've just sold a singing frog for a hundred pounds? It must have been worth millions!"

"Nah," says the guy. "The hamster is also a ventriloquist."

What's more dangerous than being with a fool?
Fooling with a bee!

What do you get if you cross a cat with a canary?
Shredded tweet!

What do you call a Russian flea?
A Moscow-ito!

What do you get if you cross an elephant with a whale?
A submarine with a built-in snorkel!

What were the only creatures not to go into the Ark in pairs?
The maggots, they went in an apple!

If you get referees in football and umpires in tennis, what do you get in bowls?
Goldfish!

What time is it when an elephant sits on your fence?
New fence time!

What would you do if an elephant sat in front of you at the movies?
Miss most of the film!

What do you get if you cross a shark with a parrot?
An animal that talks your head off!

What wobbles and eats peanuts?
Jelly the Elephant!

What's grey, has a wand, huge wings and gives money to elephants?
The tusk fairy!

Why do you need a licence for a dog and not for a cat?
Cats can't drive!

What's worse than raining cats and dogs?
Hailing taxis!

Why did the cat join the Red Cross?
Because she wanted to be a first-aid kit!

Why did Mickey Mouse get shot?
Because Donald Ducked!

What do polar bears have for lunch?
Ice burgers!

How does a bird with a broken wing manage to land safely?
With a sparrowchute!

What do bees chew?
Bumble gum!

Why did the muddy chicken cross the road twice?
He was a dirty double crosser!

What do you call a cheerful frog?
A hop-timist!

Why did the cat sleep under the car?
Because she wanted to wake up oily!

**What is the difference between a
fly and a bird?**
A bird can fly but a fly can't bird!

**What should you give a
nervous elephant?**
Trunquillizers!

Waiter, there's a fly in my soup!
What do you want for 85p, an ostrich?

What book tells you all about chickens?
A hencyclopaedia!

**How do you make a statue of
an elephant?**
Take a piece of rock and carve away
everything that doesn't look like
an elephant!

The Brave Pig

A man is visiting a farm when he notices a pig with only three legs. When he meets the farmer, he asks him how the pig came to be so disabled.

"That pig is a marvel," said the farmer, "an absolute gem. He once saved my chickens from a couple of foxes! He heard a noise one night and saw the foxes about to get through the fence and scared them off by banging a wooden spoon on a bucket." "That's amazing," said the man. "Did the foxes bite off his leg?" "No, no," said the farmer, "I tell you, that pig is worth his weight in gold. He once stopped burglars robbing my house. We were all out in the village one day and armed burglars broke into the house. He dialled 999 and let the tyres down on their car. The police caught them and recovered all our stuff." "Good Lord!" said the man. "But tell me, how did he lose the leg?

continued overleaf

Did the burglars shoot him?" "No, no, no," said the farmer, his eyes filling with tears, "I tell you, that pig is an angel sent from above. Do you know he saved my daughter's life? She was only six years old and she fell asleep in the barn one evening while feeding the new lambs with their bottle by lamplight. The lamp fell over and set fire to some hay, and before you know it the whole place was in flames. That pig went into the blazing barn and pulled my daughter out. Then he went back in eight more times and rescued every single lamb as well!" "Incredible!" said the man. "And he lost his leg in the fire?" "No, no, no," said the farmer. "THEN HOW DID HE LOSE HIS LEG?!" said the exasperated man.

"Well," said the farmer, "when you have a pig as truly exceptional as that... you don't want to eat him all at once, do you?"

There were four cats in a boat, one jumped out. How many were left?
None. They were all copy cats!

What did one flea say to the other after a night out?
Shall we walk home or take a dog?

What is worse than finding a maggot in your apple?
Finding half a maggot!

What's got eight legs and can fly long distances?
Four geese!

What do you call a flea on the moon?
A lunar-tick!

What do you give an elephant that's going to be sick?
Plenty of space!

What is the difference between a cat and a comma?
One has the paws before the claws
and the other has the clause
before the pause.

What do you get if you cross a parrot with a centipede?
A walkie-talkie!

What chases the Roadrunner and sings disco pop tunes?
Kylie Coyote!

Where do birds meet for coffee?
In a nest-café!

What do you call a crate of ducks?
A box of quackers!

What is a parrot's favourite game?
Hide and Speak!

What happens when a bomb goes off in the middle of a herd of cows?
Udder destruction!

How can you tell which end of a worm is which?
Tickle it in the middle and see which end laughs!

What is the best advice to give to a worm?
Sleep late!

What is an asset?
A small donkey!

Two hunters find some tracks in the forest.
"Those are bear tracks," said one.
"No way, those are moose tracks," said the other.
And then they were run over by a train...

What do you get if you cross an elephant and a kangaroo?

Great big holes all over Australia!

Harry was trying to smuggle a skunk out of America to sell it abroad; he asks his friend the best way to do it. "Just stick it down your trousers," his friend said. "He won't bite unless you sit on him." "But what about the terrible smell?" said Harry. His friend thought for a moment. "He'll get used to it eventually!"

What is out of bounds?
A knackered kangaroo!

What did the bee say to the flower?
Hi honey!

What do you get if your budgie flies into the blender?
Shredded Tweet!

How do you start a firefly race?
Ready Steady Glow!

What did the spider say to the bee?
Your honey or your life!

What do cows play at parties?
Moo-sical chairs!

The Mighty Tiger

A tiger corners a monkey one day and roars: "WHO IS THE MIGHTIEST OF ALL THE JUNGLE ANIMALS?" The poor monkey replies: "You, of course! No-one is mightier than you, Tiger!" A little while later the tiger finds a deer, and bellows out: "WHO IS THE MIGHTIEST OF ALL THE JUNGLE ANIMALS?" The deer is shaking so hard it can barely speak, but manages to squeak: "Oh Great Tiger, you are the mightiest animal in the jungle!" The tiger, feeling good, swaggers up to a female elephant that is quietly eating some weeds. He roars: "WHO IS THE MIGHTIEST OF ALL THE JUNGLE ANIMALS?" The elephant grabs the tiger with her trunk, slams him down, picks him up again, and shakes him until his teeth rattle. Finally she throws him hard

into a nearby tree. The tiger staggers to his feet and looks at the elephant and says:
"Just because you don't know the answer, you don't have to get so upset..."

What happens when ducks fly upside down?
They quack up!

What's grey on the inside and clear on the outside?
An elephant in a plastic bag!

What do frogs eat with their hamburgers?
French flies!

Why do elephants wear sandals?
To keep from sinking into the sand!

Why do ostriches stick their heads in the sand?
To look for elephants that weren't wearing sandals!

What happened to the hyena that swallowed an Oxo cube?
He made a laughing stock of himself!

What did the woodworm say to the chair?
It's been nice gnawing you!

What happened when the owl lost his voice?
He didn't give a hoot!

What do you get when you cross a python with a porcupine?
Ten feet of barbed wire!

What do you call a cat who does tricks?
A magic kit!

How do you get two whales in a Nissan Micra?
Straight up the M4 and over the Severn Bridge. (To Wales.)

How do you get four elephants in a Nissan Micra?

Two in the front, two in the back!

How do you recognise an elephant's house?

There's a Nissan Micra outside!

Two monkeys had a dare, to paint a lion's bottom blue as he slept. Bobby monkey crept up to the sleeping beast and carefully painted its hindquarters, but suddenly the lion woke up. Bobby shot off like a hare, being chased by the angry lion. Through the jungle they sped, until Bobby jumped over the wall to a house. Quickly, he sat in a garden chair and pulled a newspaper over his face. The enraged lion wasn't far behind: he came leaping over the wall and stopped in front of the trembling monkey. "Did you see a monkey come through here?" said the lion. "What?" said Bobby, still shaking. "The one that painted that lion's bum blue?"
"Oh no!" said the lion. "Don't tell me it's in the papers already!"

How do you make an elephant stew?
You keep it waiting for a few hours!

How can you tell an elephant from a giraffe?
Say "Hi giraffe" and if it doesn't answer, it's probably an elephant!

I went to the dentist yesterday. He said, "Say Aaah." I said, "Why?"
He said, "My dog's died."

What looks like a horse and flies?
A flying horse!

Who clucked and conquered half the world?
Attila the Hen!

What did the buffalo say when his son went on holiday?
Bison!

How do you find out how many cows you have?
With a pocket cowculator!

What part of a fish weighs the most?
The scales!

What did the banana do when the monkey chased it?
The banana split!

Farmer Brown meets his friend in the village pub. "Harold, what did you give your bull when it had colic?" "Vinegar and Fairy Liquid," said Harold. A week later they met again. Farmer Brown says, "Oi, Harold! I gave my bull vinegar and Fairy Liquid, like you said, and it died!"
"So did mine!" said Harold.

Which dinosaur had one leg?
All of them!

What do you get when you cross a cow and a duck?
Cheese and quackers!

Why don't owls sing when it is raining?

Cos it's too wet to woo!

The Rude Parrot 2

A lady was walking to work and she saw a parrot on a perch in front of a pet shop. The parrot shouted,"Oi! You're really ugly!" Well, the lady was furious! She stormed past the shop to her work. Going home that night, she saw the same parrot and it said, "Oi! You're really ugly!" She was very angry. She went into the shop and told the owners that she was going to sue them and have the bird put down if they didn't make it stop insulting her. The owners told her they would make sure he didn't do it again. The next morning, she again passed in front of the shop. The parrot was still on his perch. When she walked by, the parrot said, "Oi!" She stopped and turned to the parrot and said, "Yes, what?" The parrot looked at her and said: "You know..."

What is white, sugary, has whiskers and floats?
A catameringue!

What did the slug say as he slipped down the wall?
How slime flies!

What is the difference between fleas and dogs?
Dogs can have fleas but fleas can't have dogs!

What did the clean dog say to the insect?
Long time no flea!

What goes clomp, clomp, clomp, squish; clomp, clomp, clomp, squish?
An elephant with one wet shoe!

What happened when 500 hares got loose on the main street?
The police had to comb the area!

**A vicar was reading Bible stories
to his Sunday school class. He read:
"The man named Lot was warned to
take his wife and flee out of the city,
but his wife looked back
and was turned into a pillar of salt."**
One of the children asked,
"What happened to the flea?"

**What became of the man who was
swallowed by a cow?**
He became the man in the moo!

What do you give a dog with a fever?
Mustard, it's the best thing for a hot dog!

Why do baby giraffes walk softly?
Because they can't walk hardly!

What does an elf get in a cow field?
A pat on the head!

What do you get if you cross a pig and a laundry?

Hogwash!

Teacher: If I gave you three rabbits today and five rabbits tomorrow, how many rabbits would you have?
Jackie: Nine.
Teacher: That's not right, you'd have eight.
Jackie: No, I'd have nine. I already have one rabbit at home!

What did the fish say when he swam into the wall?
Dam!

What do you call a story about young horses?
A pony tail!

Why don't you see elephants in lifts?
Because they hide in the back corners!

Why do elephants drink so much?
To try to forget!

A vicar is buying a parrot.
"Are you sure it doesn't scream, yell, or swear?" asked the preacher.
"Oh absolutely. It's a religious parrot," the shopkeeper assured him. "Do you see those strings on his legs? When you pull the right one, he recites the Lord's Prayer, and when you pull on the left he recites the 23rd Psalm." "Wonderful!" says the preacher. "But what happens if you pull both strings?"
"I fall off my perch, you fool!" screeched the parrot.

Two fleas were running across the top of a cereal packet.
"Why are we running so fast?" said one.
"Because it says 'Tear along the dotted line!'"

Why should you never buy dogs that are going cheap?
Because a healthy dog should go "Woof"!

The Talking Dog

A man and his dog walk into a bar.
The man says to the barman:
"I'll bet you a round of drinks that my
dog can talk." The bartender says, "Yeah!
Sure...go ahead." The man says to his
dog, "What covers a house?" and his dog
says, "Roof!" The man says, "How does
sandpaper feel?" and the dog says,
"Rough!"

The man asks, "What percentage of the
Earth's surface is water?"
and the dog says, "Arf!"
"There!" said the man.
"I told you he could talk!"
The bartender, annoyed at this point,
throws both of them out the door.
Sitting on the pavement,
the dog looks at the man and says,
"Or is it three-quarters?"

What's big, white and scary with a hole in the middle?
A polo bear!

What do you get if you cross a frog with a traffic warden?
Toad away!

Why did King Kong climb the Empire State Building?
Because he couldn't fit in the lift!

What's pink and grey and has four feet?
A hippopotamus poking its tongue out!

Rachel: How did you like the parrot I sent you?
Michele: It was delicious!
Rachel: You ate it? I paid 500 dollars for that parrot, and it spoke seven different languages!
Michele: Then why didn't it say anything when I put it in the oven?!

Who took ten thousand pigs up a hill?
The Grand Old Duke of Pork!

Who steals soap from the bath?
Robber ducks!

A magician was working on a cruise ship performing tricks for the guests. But his act was ruined every night by the captain's parrot, who would shout out, "It's up your sleeve!" or "She's gone through the hidden trapdoor!" during his act, and give the tricks away. Unfortunately, the ship struck an iceberg one night and the magician and the parrot ended up in the same lifeboat. After a week of silence, the parrot turned to the magician and said,

"All right, I give up - what did you do with the ship?"

What should you do if you are on a picnic with King Kong?

Give him the biggest bananas!

How do you stop a cockerel crowing on Sunday morning?

Have him for lunch on Saturday!

The Antique Saucer

A famous art collector is walking through the city when he notices an old cat lapping milk from a saucer in the doorway of a shop.
He notices that the saucer is extremely old and very, very valuable.
So he walks casually into the store and offers to buy the cat for £2. The shopkeeper replies, "I'm sorry, but the cat isn't for sale."
The collector says, "Please, I need a hungry cat around the house to catch mice.
I'll pay you £20 for him."
And the shopkeeper says, "Sold!" and hands over the cat. The collector continues,
"Hey, for the 20 quid I wonder if you could throw in that old saucer? The cat's used to it and it'll save mc from
having to get a dish."
And the shopkeeper says,
"Sorry, Mate, but that's my lucky saucer.
So far this week I've sold 68 cats!"

**What happened when the cat ate
a ball of wool?**
She had mittens!

**Customer: I'll take this parrot. Could you
please send me the bill?**
Shopkeeper: I'm sorry, but you'll have to
take the whole bird!

**What do you get when you cross a pig
and a centipede?**
Bacon and legs!

**A Ring-Tailed Lemur goes into a tea shop
and orders a jam scone.
"That'll be £2.50 please, Sir,"
said the waitress.
"I must say, we don't get many
Ring-Tailed Lemurs in here!"**
"I'm not surprised," said the Lemur.
"Two and a half quid for a scone?!"

What's grey and squirts jam at you?
A mouse eating a doughnut!

What do you get if you pour boiling water down a rabbit hole?
Hot cross bunnies!

What has six ears, twelve legs and can't watch telly?
Three blind mice!

The Bragging Horses

Some racehorses are chatting in a stable. One of them starts to boast about his track record: "In the last 15 races I've run, I've won 8 of them!" "That's nothing!" another horse breaks in, "In the last 27 races I've run, I've won 19!" "Oh that's not bad," says another, flicking his tail, "but in the last 36 races I've run, I've won 28!" At this point, they notice that a greyhound dog has been sitting there listening. "I don't mean to boast," says the greyhound, "but in my last 104 races, I've won 103 of them." The horses are clearly amazed. "Wow!" says one, after a hushed silence. "A talking dog!"

Why does an ostrich have such a long neck?
Because its head is so far from its body!

How can you tell when your dog is stupid?
He keeps barking up the wrong tree!

What do giraffes have that no other animal has?
Baby giraffes!

My dog likes to sit down each evening and surf the Internet.
Wow! What a smart animal!
Not really, it took the cat three weeks to teach him!

What do we get from naughty cows?
Bad milk!

Why did the dinosaur cross the road?
Because chickens weren't invented then!

What do you get if you cross a cow and a jogging machine?
A milk shake!

A Chihuahua, a Doberman and a Bulldog are in a doggie bar having a drink when a good-looking girl Poodle comes up to them and says, "Whoever can say 'liver and cheese' in the best sentence can go out on a date with me." So the Doberman says, "I love liver and cheese." The Poodle says, "That's not good enough!" The Bulldog says, "I hate liver and cheese." She says, "That's not good enough either!"
Finally, the Chihuahua says, "Liver alone... cheese mine!"

How do you stop an elephant from going through the eye of a needle?
Tie a knot in its tail!

Why did the ram run over the cliff?
He didn't see the ewe turn!

What's the loudest pet you can have?
A trumpet!

The Escaped Gorilla

A gorilla escapes from the zoo and after three weeks, the zoo keepers give up looking for him. Some time later, a man calls the zoo complaining of a gorilla in a tree in his back yard. The zoo keeper rushes right over. When he arrives, he has a net, a baseball bat, a shotgun, and a huge dog. The man asks what the items are for. He's told, "I'm gonna climb the tree and hit the gorilla in the head with the baseball bat. When he falls out of the tree, you throw the net over him. The dog will go straight for his bum and bite it really hard." The man asks, "But what's the shotgun for?" The zoo keeper answers, "If I miss the gorilla and fall out of the tree, you shoot the dog..."

What goes dot-dot-dash-dash-squeak?
Mouse code!

A guy went into a police station and put a dead cat on the counter. "Somebody threw this into my front garden!" he complained. "Alright, sir," said the officer.
"Come back in six months and if no-one's claimed it, it's yours!"

What did the giant canary say?
TWEET!

What do greedy fish eat?
Everyfin!

What has six legs and flies?
An airline pilot with a cat!

What does a cat go to sleep on?
A caterpillar!

Why was night cricket invented?
Because bats like to sleep in the daytime!

Why did the turkey cross the road?
It was the chicken's day off!

The Jungle Violinist

**A famous violinist is canoeing up a river in Africa when he hits a rock and is forced to swim for shore. Soon he is surrounded by 40 hungry, snarling jungle beasts, from tigers and hyenas to huge man-eating snakes. The animals advance towards the musician, drooling. Thinking quickly, he whips out his violin and begins to play.
Sure enough, the animals are so bewitched by the music that they stop snarling and sit down to listen.
Presently an old crocodile emerges from the river, shuffles straight up to the violinist and eats him.**

"Hey!" said a lion, "What are you doing? We were enjoying that!"
"PARDON?!" says the crocodile...

A woman is thinking about buying a mink coat. "Will it be all right in the rain?" she asked the shop assistant.
"Have you ever seen a mink with an umbrella?" he said.

Two sheep meet on a country lane. The first one says, "Baa!" The second one says, "Woof!" "What are you up to? Sheep don't go 'Woof'." said the first sheep.
"I'm sorry," said the second, "I'm new round here."

Why did the antelope?
Nobody gnu!

Why did the pelican refuse to pay for his meal?
His bill was too big!

What always goes to bed with shoes on?
A horse!

Tony, who lives in the city, asks a farmer: "Why doesn't this cow have any horns?"
Farmer: "There are many reasons: some cows are born without horns, some cows shed their horns, some cows have their horns taken out. But as for this cow here, the reason is simple. It's a horse."

What do you get if you cross a road with a safari park?
Double yellow lions!

A girl finds a frog in the woods. "Excuse me, young lady," says the frog, "I'm not really a frog, I'm a Prince! Kiss me and you will return me to my real form!"
"No thanks," said the girl.
"Princes are two a penny, but a talking frog? I'm going to make a packet!"

How do lobsters travel around?
Taxi crab!

How do you teach a dog to fetch?
Tie a cat to a stick!

What did the triceratops wear on its legs?
Tricerabottoms!

Why did the Tyrannosaurus stand in the corner?
Because he'd been naughty!

What lies on the ground 100 feet up in the air?
A dead caterpillar!

A bloke goes into a pub with a giraffe, they both get drunk and the giraffe collapses in a heap on the floor. The bloke goes to leave and the barman says, "Hey! You can't leave that lying on the floor!"
The bloke says:
"It's not a lion, it's a giraffe."

A Tasmanian wide-mouthed frog

This joke requires the teller to make two special faces!

The toad's speaking face.

The punch-line face.

Once, a Tasmanian wide-mouthed frog decided to leave Tasmania and see the world. After a long journey over land and sea, he found himself in Africa...

continued overleaf

Everything was new and exciting to him, and he was full of questions. He met a giraffe and said, "Wow! You're so tall, what are you?" "I'm a giraffe," said the giraffe. "Hello! I'm a Tasmanian wide-mouthed frog! What do giraffes eat?" said the Tasmanian wide-mouthed frog. "Oh, I eat leaves and fruit, mainly," said the giraffe. The frog said goodbye and hopped off. Next he came across a zebra. "Wow!" he said. "A stripey horse!" "No. I'm a zebra," said the zebra. "Hello! I'm a Tasmanian wide-mouthed frog! What do zebras eat?" said the Tasmanian wide-mouthed frog. "Oh, I eat grass, mainly," said the zebra. The frog said goodbye and hopped off. Soon, he came upon a great, big lion. "Wow!" said the Tasmanian wide-mouthed frog. "What are you?!"
"I'm a lion," said the lion.

"Wow!" said the frog. "And what do lions eat?" The lion looked him right in the eye. "We eat Tasmanian wide-mouthed frogs," said the lion. "Oh..," said the frog,

"I don't suppose you get many of those round here, do you?"

Two guys are out hiking. All of a sudden, a bear starts chasing them. They climb a tree, but the bear starts climbing up the tree after them. The first guy gets his trainers out of his knapsack and starts putting them on. The second guy says, "What are you doing?" He says: "I figure when the bear gets close to us, we'll jump down and make a run for it." The second guy says: "Are you crazy? You can't run faster than a bear!" The first guy says: "I don't have to run faster than the bear. I only have to run faster than you!"

Baby skunk: Can I have a chemistry set for my birthday?
Mummy Skunk: No.
Baby Skunk: Why not?
Mummy Skunk: Because I don't want you stinking the house out!

What's grey, yellow, grey, yellow, grey, yellow, grey, yellow, grey, yellow, grey, yellow?
An elephant rolling down a hill with a daisy in its mouth.

What do you call it when a frog takes a shower?
Spring cleaning!

A horse, a monkey, a vicar, an Englishman, an Irishman, a Scotsman, a Rabbi, a hamster, a clown and a blonde all walk into a bar together.
The barman turns to them and says:
"Is this some kind of a joke?"

A naughty young chick is being told off by his angry Mum.
"If your father could see you now," said Mother Hen, "he'd turn over in his gravy!"

A fireman is working on the engine outside the station when he notices a little girl next door in a little red wagon with little ladders hung off the side and a garden hose tightly coiled in the middle. The girl is wearing a fireman's helmet and has the wagon tied to a dog and cat. The fireman walks over to take a closer look. "That's a nice fire engine," the fireman says with admiration. "Thanks," the girl says. The fireman looks a little closer and notices the girl has tied the wagon to the dog's collar and to the cat's tail. "Excuse me, Miss," the fire fighter says, "I don't want to tell you how to run your fire engine, but if you were to tie that rope around the cat's collar, I think you could go faster." The little girl replied, "You're probably right, but then I wouldn't have a siren."

What kind of ties do pigs wear?

Pig stys!

A man goes into a pet shop and tells the owner that he wants to buy a pet that can do everything. The shop owner suggests a faithful dog. The man replies, "Come on, a dog?" The owner says, "How about a cat?" The man replies, "No way! A cat certainly can't do everything. I want a pet that can do everything!" The shop owner thinks for a minute, then says, "I've got it! A centipede!" The man says, "A centipede? I can't imagine a centipede doing everything, but okay... I'll try a centipede." He gets the centipede home and says to the centipede, "Clean the kitchen." Thirty minutes later, he walks into the kitchen and... it's immaculate! All the dishes have been washed, dried, and put away; the counter-tops cleaned; the appliances sparkling; the floor waxed. He's amazed. He says to the centipede, "Clean the living room."

The world's funniest ANIMAL JOKES

106

Twenty minutes later, he walks into the living room. The carpet has been vacuumed; the furniture cleaned and dusted; the pillows on the sofa plumped; the plants watered.

The man thinks to himself, "This is the most amazing thing I've ever seen. This really is a pet that can do everything!" Next he says to the centipede, "Run down to the corner and get me a newspaper." The centipede walks out the door. Ten minutes later... no centipede. Twenty minutes later... no centipede. Thirty minutes later... no centipede. By this point the man is wondering what's going on. The centipede should have been back in a couple of minutes. Forty-five minutes later... still no centipede! So he goes to the front door, opens it ... and there's the centipede sitting right outside. The man says, "Hey! I sent you down to the corner shop 45 minutes ago to get me a newspaper. What's the matter?!"

The centipede says, "I'm goin'! I'm goin'! I'm just puttin' on my shoes!"

What would you get if Batman and Robin were run over by a herd of stampeding elephants?
Flatman and Ribbon!

What does it mean when the Easter Bunny arrives one day late with melted chocolate?
He probably had a bad hare day.

Why do hens lay eggs?
If they dropped them, they'd break!

A leopard went to see an optician because he thought he needed an eye exam. "Every time I look at my wife," he worriedly told the optician, "I see spots before my eyes." "So what's to worry about?" replied the doctor. "You're a leopard, aren't you?" "What's that got to do with anything?" replied the patient. "My wife is a zebra!"

Two fish were in a tank.
One says to the other,
"So, how do you drive this thing?"

It's a sunny morning in the Big Forest and the Bear family are just waking up. Baby Bear goes downstairs and sits in his small chair at the table.
He looks into his small bowl. It is empty!
"Who's been eating my porridge?!" he squeaks. Daddy Bear arrives at the table and sits in his big chair. He looks into his big bowl. It is also empty!
"Who's been eating my porridge?!" he roars. Mummy Bear puts her head through the serving hatch from the kitchen and screams,
"For Pete's sake, how many times do we have to go through this? I haven't made the stupid porridge yet!"

How does a rabbit make gold soup?
He begins with 24 carrots.

What did the frog order at McDonald's?
French flies and a diet Croak!

A mother and baby camel are talking one day when the baby camel asks, "Mum, why have I got these huge three-toed feet?" The mother replies, "Well son, when we trek across the desert your toes will help you to stay on top of the soft sand." "OK," said the son. A few minutes later the son asks, "Mum, why have I got these great long eyelashes?" "They are there to keep the sand out of your eyes on the trips through the desert." "I see," replies the son. After a short while, the son returns and asks, "Mum, why have I got these great big humps on my back?" The mother, now a little impatient with the boy replies, "They are there to help us store water for our long treks across the desert, so we can survive without eating and drinking for long periods of time!" "That's great, Mum, so we have huge feet to stop us sinking, and long eyelashes to keep the sand from our eyes and these humps to store water, but Mum..." "What now!?"

"Why are we in London Zoo?"

How does a frog feel when he has a broken leg?
Very unhoppy!

How do you hide an elephant in a box of Smarties?
Paint his toenails all different colours!

Hank heard a shot, followed by howling and another shot.
He ran next door and found his friend Tony crying.
"Say, what's wrong?" Hank asked.
Tony sobbed, "I had to shoot my dog."
Hank said, "My God! Was he mad?"
Tony replied,
"Well, he wasn't too happy about it."

A country dog, coming to the city and seeing his first parking meter, thinks,
"How do you like that? Pay toilets!"

What did the duck say when he'd finished shopping?
Put it on my bill please!

Hallowe'n

How do you keep an elephant from stampeding?
Take his stampeder away!

One night, two vampire bats were hanging upside down in a cave. One says, "Hey, you wanna go and get some blood?" and the other bat says, "Where are we going to get blood at two in the morning?"
So the other bat says, "You don't want to go? Fine, I'll go by myself!"
And off he flapped. About 30 minutes later, the first bat came back with fresh blood dripping out of his mouth and all over his body.
The second bat says, "Hey, where did you get all that blood?"
The first bat says, "See that tree over there?"
"Yeah," says the second bat..
"Well I didn't," said the first bat.

If you enjoyed this book, you can find more hilarious jokes, amazing facts, and brainbusting riddles and puzzles in the following books, also published by Dean:

Title	ISBN
The World's Funniest Disgusting Jokes for Kids	0 603 56065 2
The World's Funniest School Jokes for Kids	0 603 56063 6
The World's Most Amazing Animal Facts for Kids	0 603 56060 1
The World's Most Amazing Planet Earth Facts for Kids	0 603 56062 8
The World's Most Amazing Science Facts for Kids	0 603 56061X
1000 of the World's Funniest Jokes for Kids	0 603 56066 0
1000 of the World's Most Astonishing Facts for Kids	0 603 56067 9
1000 of the World's Greatest Brainbusters	0 603 56068 7